Disney Christmas Magic

The Ultimate Insider's Guide to Spending the Holidays at Walt Disney World

By

Roger Wilk

Copyright Notice

© 2013 Roger Wilk

Table of Contents

1) Christmas at Disney

Imagine the happiest place on Earth. Hundreds of acres of impeccably kept grounds filled with magical memories and good times. Tons of great rides and attractions to keep you busy for hours on end. Fantastic shows to bring a smile to every face in every place. Imagine experiences that will create joyous memories to last a lifetime.

Magic Kingdom is even MORE MAGICAL at Christmas!

Imagine a grand castle aglow with thousands of dancing lights. Imagine the lush tropical landscapes and thousands of helpful 'cast members' whose only goal is to make sure you have a fantastic time. Imagine the thrills and chills of the most amazing theme parks on the planet. Take in the aroma of delicious cinnamon rolls and other delectable baked goods wafting down Main Street, U.S.A. as you pass by the bakery. Envision the sights and sounds of some of the coolest parades ever. Imagine the fireworks and other pyrotechnics of some of the most amazing nighttime shows you'll ever see. Got it?

Now take all of those things you've imagined at the happiest place on Earth and imagine them during the most magical, wonderful, spectacular season of the year- the Christmas season!

The Magical entrance to The Magic Kingdom during the Christmas season

Imagine replacing the beautiful flowering plants that adorn these impeccable landscapes with thousands of Christmas poinsettias, ribbons, and bows. Imagine festive wreaths adorning every lamppost and streetlight. Imagine MILLIONS of dancing holiday lights synchronized to your favorite holiday music. Imagine your favorite Disney characters all decked out in holiday cheer. Imagine the glorious castle- now even more stunning with holiday lights galore and a special, HUGE projection show.

Envision yourself and your family in the front row on Main Street, U.S.A. at Magic Kingdom, witnessing one of the most amazing Christmas parades ever! Imagine enjoying fresh-baked cookies at one of the coolest Christmas parties ever!

If you're thinking of going to Walt Disney World in Orlando for the Christmas season, all I can say is DO IT!!! Although the Christmas season is one of the busiest times of the year for Walt Disney World and The Magic Kingdom, it's busy for a reason. It's the one time of year "The Happiest Place on Earth" can become **EVEN MORE MAGICAL THAN EVER!**

Main Street, U.S.A. decked out for Christmas at The Magic Kingdom

If you've already booked a trip to Walt Disney World during the Holiday Season, or if you're even just thinking about it, **THIS** book is the **RIGHT** book for you! Christmas at Walt Disney World is an experience you won't want to miss. In this book, I'll show you how to make the most of your trip- and your time at Disney. The holiday season is a festive and very crowded time of year at Walt Disney World. It's also a time filled with special events, decorations, and other festivities to make it a memorable experience. AND believe it or not, you CAN avoid the crowds (at least some of the time) if you plan your trip carefully!

Reasons to go to Disney at Christmas

- The "Happiest Place on Earth" is even MORE MAGICAL during the Christmas season!
- The weather! If you've been to Disney in the summer, you know what a steamy hot oven Orlando can be that time of year. Imagine a vacation where you're not sweating your butt off the whole time!
- Disney plans lots of special events over the holiday season that you won't find any other time of year.
- The decorations in the parks make a beautiful place even more spectacular.
- Two words: Osborne Lights!
- If you're from a cold weather climate it will be a nice break from cold, snowy, winter weather.

Reasons to avoid Disney at Christmas

- Christmas week through New Year's Eve is CRAZY CROWDED!
- The weather! December and January are the coolest months in Orlando with average highs

in the low 70s and lows in the 50s. If you're there when a cold front goes through it can be much colder!
- Rental cars, flights, and hotels can be much more expensive.
- You could be home playing with all your Christmas presents.

Holiday Weather at Disney

Last year was our first visit to Disney during the holiday season- and it definitely won't be our last. We've been to Walt Disney World several times in the heat of the summer, and this was quite a change! During our summer visits we'd load up on bottled water and those little 'spray fans'. For our family of five, we'd bring 3-4 fans, and usually lugged around 5-7 20oz. bottled waters. We'd go through a few gallons of water throughout the day. This time, we still carried some water just for convenience, but we rarely needed it. We didn't even think of bringing our spray fans. That part was really great!

During much of our trip, we wandered around the parks of Walt Disney World in complete comfort. Although we needed jeans and long-sleeved shirts on some days, it was still a pleasant break from the summer heat that we had grown accustomed to. Even when the days are warm this time of year, the nights can be pretty chilly. You may be in short sleeves and shorts during the day, and need hoodies and long pants at night.

Orlando, FL Average Temps

Month	High (F)	Low (F)	High (C)	Low (C)	Humidity (1pm)	Rain (Inches)
December	74	52	24	11	57%	2.2"
January	73	48	22	11	56%	2.2"

The downside of visiting Disney during December and January is the weather can still get pretty chilly. You may have a few days in the low 80's, and then a cold front moves through and Brrrrrrr.... We had a couple of days that were downright COLD! On Tuesday, the third day of our trip, the HIGH was about 48 and it was very windy. We're just not used to hearing talk of freeze warnings and wind chills in the 30s in Orlando. We were bundled up in gloves and a few layers of sweatshirts, and we were wishing we would have brought winter coats!

When packing for a Disney Christmas vacation, you'll need to pack clothes for just about any weather. Dress in layers and be prepared for anything!

Be prepared for an occasional cold front during Christmas at Disney

2) Disney Christmas Overview

The 'Christmas Season' begins right after Thanksgiving in late November and lasts until the week after New Year's when the Christmas decorations are finally taken down. The dates may vary depending on how the calendar falls.

In Christmas 2012, the Christmas decorations began to 'magically' disappear on January 7th, 2013. The last day for the 'The Osborne Family Spectacle of Dancing Lights or 'Osborne Lights' was Sunday, January 6th. Check the official Walt Disney World events calendar for the exact dates of all the special events held during the Christmas season.

Osborne Lights- a great reason to visit Disney at Christmas!

Depending on which week you decide to go, some of the events may have already been completed for the season. EPCOT's 'Holidays Around The World - Candlelight Processional' for example only runs through December 30th so if you go the week following New Year's you'll miss it. Mickey's Very Merry Christmas Party at Magic Kingdom only runs on select evenings through December 21st, so if you arrive at Disney after that, you won't get to enjoy that wonderful experience. Even if you miss out on these events, you'll still get to enjoy lots of other Christmas events, decorations, and festivities during your stay.

No matter when you go during the holiday season, your experience will be a little different than at other times of the year. Here's an overview of what you can expect to be different during Christmas at Walt Disney World.

Disney Water Parks at Christmas

Depending on your priorities, you may want to skip the water parks altogether on your Christmas visit to Walt Disney World. Winter months are the best time for maintenance on the various water slides and other water park attractions, so many attractions will be closed. One of the parks is usually closed completely for maintenance, and the park that stays open will have reduced hours- closing by 5:00 p.m. each day.

Disney water parks will be less crowded than usual

With the weather being 'iffy' this time of year, you may end up wasting your money if you buy the 'Water Parks, fun and more' option on your pre-purchased Disney tickets. Sure, you can still use this option to play golf or visit DisneyQuest, but if the weather is not great for the wave pools and waterslides of Blizzard Beach or Typhoon Lagoon, you may feel that you didn't get your money's worth.

The Water Park Fun & More option add-on to your theme park tickets may still be a good option for your family- if you're prepared to enjoy the '& more' portion of the ticket should the weather not be warm enough for a tumble down the water slides. If you'd enjoy visits to DisneyQuest, or the various other options just as much, by all means give it a shot.

If you really hope to check out the water parks, another possibility would be to wait and see how the weather is, then purchase a one-day pass if the weather is warm. This may be a bit pricey, but at least you won't spend money on days and visits that you don't use. To learn more about the water parks option, and other options available for your Disney tickets, check out my first book, **Discover the Magic: The Ultimate Insider's Guide to Walt Disney World**. That book has a whole section on the water parks and a section on all the Disney ticket options too!

Christmas Crowds

If you've done any research, you know that the week between Christmas and New Year's is probably the busiest of the year, and last year's Christmas season was no exception. New Year's Eve was the busiest ever, and the parks (especially Magic Kingdom) can get so crowded that sometimes they have to close the park to new guests! If you plan to visit the parks between Christmas and New Year's, be prepared...and be patient. You won't get to ride all the rides you want and you won't be able to do all the things you want to do. If you can accept that, you're sure to still have a good time.

Expect major crowds during Christmas vacation

If your first visit to Walt Disney World is during the Christmas season, you may be shocked at just how crowded the parks can get. Just relax and enjoy the atmosphere- and don't be in a hurry to get anywhere! Main Street, U.S.A. at Magic Kingdom will be wall to wall people for most of the day, so it will take a bit of time to make your way down the street.

You'll wait in longer lines at every attraction- especially the most popular ones like Toy Story Mania at Hollywood Studios, Space Mountain at Magic Kingdom, or Test Track and Soarin' at Epcot. Use FASTPASSES to your advantage to make the most of your day.

If you've been to Disney during one of the peak seasons other than Christmas, you pretty much know what to expect. The peak times at Christmas will be more crowded than even the peak of the summer season, so it will be more crowded than you've ever seen it. However, you'll have the advantage of the cooler weather so rather than melting in the scorching Florida summer sun, you'll be pleasantly comfortable. That will make handling the crowds a bit easier.

Not so crowded times during the busy season

So what do you do if you want to visit Magic Kingdom and the rest of the parks at Christmastime so you can enjoy the 'holiday atmosphere' and all the Christmas decorations and special events, but you do NOT want to deal with the crazy crowds? The good news is there ARE times you can go where the crowds won't be terrible AND you can still enjoy the Christmas decorations and MOST of the special Christmas events at Magic Kingdom, Epcot, Animal Kingdom and Hollywood Studios.

Certain times during Christmas will be less crowded than others

If you want to enjoy the Christmas festivities at Walt Disney World without the craziest crowds, consider traveling to Orlando during the first couple of weeks of December. You'll find the crowds considerably smaller during this time, and you're more likely to have warmer weather too. Plus, you'll be back home with plenty of time left to finish your Christmas shopping!

Can the kids miss school for a Disney trip?

If you're debating whether to take the kids out of school for the trip, you'll need to decide whether it is worth it for you. Personally, I think if the kids are younger it's definitely worth it! If the kids miss a week of school, they'll definitely have to play 'catch up' for all they've missed, but I think the magical memories you'll have from your trip will definitely make it worthwhile!

If you have a high-schooler, your decision becomes a bit more complicated. For most schools, mid-December is getting near the end of a report card marking period or semester. You certainly don't want to hurt your child's chance of getting into a certain college because their grades dropped because the missed a week of school just before finals. That's an individual decision that you should discuss as a family.

I don't want to miss school, or face the crowds, but I want to spend the holidays at Walt Disney World. What should I do?

If you don't want to pull your kids out of school to visit Walt Disney World over the holidays, and traveling during Christmas week just won't work for you, you may still have an option. Depending on how the calendar falls, you may be able to travel the week of New Year's and avoid some of the biggest crowds, while still not missing school. (Or maybe just a couple of days.)

Disney stays decked out for Christmas until the week AFTER New Year's!

This worked out great for us in 2012. With New Year's Day on a Sunday, most businesses took Monday off as the holiday. Our kids didn't go back to school until the 9th of January. We were able to do our Disney trip by flying out early on New Year's Day and returning home on Sunday, the 8th. This worked out GREAT! We went straight from the airport to Magic Kingdom!

Although it was fairly crowded on New Year's Day, several cast members (Disney employees) told us the day before was WAY more crowded. We were able to enjoy a Magical Day at Magic Kingdom without the crush of people like the day before. Needless to say we were exhausted when we checked into our hotel around midnight, but it was well worth it!

To make it even better, the crowds diminished as the week went on. All of the parks were much less crowded than they've been during our visits in the summer months. Even though we had a couple of cold days (the HIGH on Tuesday was 48!) we had a great time! Plus we still got to enjoy most of the holiday festivities- they didn't start taking the decorations down until the day we left.

3) Magic Kingdom Christmas

The entrance to Magic Kingdom

From the time you reach the Ticket and Transportation Center (TTC) to board the monorail to Magic Kingdom, you'll know the Christmas season is in full swing at Walt Disney World. There are poinsettias EVERYWHERE! In Disney's usual creative way, this flowery symbol of Christmas welcomes you in every way imaginable.

The entrance to Magic Kingdom is equally beautiful with hundreds (thousands?) of poinsettias mixed in with garland, bows, and the usual Disney flowers and decorative plants. A huge 15' Mickey Mouse silhouette made entirely of poinsettias is the centerpiece of the main entrance.

Magic Kingdom's giant Christmas tree

Cross through the main gate to The Magic Kingdom and you'll be greeted by a giant Christmas tree surrounded by toy soldiers, candy canes, presents, and other holiday goodies. The tree is at the center of the roundabout just in front of the train station and it towers over Main Street, U.S.A. Although you'll be in a hurry to check out the rest of the park- stop! Take a minute to enjoy it. It truly is a sight to behold.

Next, head over to the left for a quick photo op with a toy soldier or with Winnie the Pooh- or should I say "Santa Pooh?" and Tigger too! There's a neat "Days Til Christmas" countdown board. After it gets to zero on Christmas Day, it starts right back up again at 365. A fun way to get in the spirit for NEXT Christmas!

Stop for a photo op with Tigger and Pooh!

The shops along Main Street, U.S.A. are beautifully decorated for the season, and the garland draped across the light poles lining the street, complete with Mickey Mouse wreaths, adds a nice touch. Many shops have Christmas window displays and all have unique Christmas souvenirs you won't find anywhere else, or at any other time of year at Walt Disney World. Cinderella Castle is also adorned for the season with thousands of extra lights complete with lots of special effects! (More on that later...)

The rest of Magic Kingdom is sprinkled with similar decorations for the season as well. You'll find smaller Christmas trees, garland, poinsettias and such throughout. Disney has a way of doing things just right- a touch a class without going into gaudy excess.

It's sometimes the little touches- like the Mickey & Minnie Mouse topiaries near Cinderella Castle, all decked out for Christmas, that make visiting The Magic Kingdom even that much more special!

Mickey & Minnie – Dressed for the holidays!

Magic Kingdom Christmas Events

Aside from the decorations, you'll find lots of fun events at Magic Kingdom- just for the holidays! Here's a look at some of the special Christmas & New Year's activities you'll find during the Christmas season at Magic Kingdom:

Mickey's Very Merry Christmas Party

Mickey's Very Merry Christmas Party is a special event held on select nights during the holiday season at Magic Kingdom. You'll need to purchase a separate ticket separate ticket (about $60) to attend. The event includes live entertainment, a unique Christmas parade down Main Street, a special fireworks show, and lots more.

"Mickey's Once Upon a Christmastime" parade

Here's a glimpse at what you can expect if you attend Mickey's special Christmas party at Magic Kingdom:

- See Cinderella Castle, aglow with special enchanted Castle Dream Lights
- A special "Mickey's Once Upon a Christmastime" parade featuring Santa Claus!

- A special "Holiday Wishes: Celebrate the Spirit of the Season" fireworks show
- Live holiday entertainment featuring your favorite Disney characters
- Complimentary hot cocoa and cookies
- A magical Christmas snowfall
- Special 'meet and greet' opportunities with your favorite Disney characters. (Some characters like the 7 dwarfs can ONLY be seen at the party.)

See Mickey, Minnie, and Santa Claus too!

The party is only held on specific nights from 7:00 p.m. – 12:00 a.m. (usually Thursday – Sunday), and there are no parties during the week between Christmas and New Year's. Be sure to check the Disney website for the schedule so you can plan your visit to Magic Kingdom accordingly. If you purchase your tickets in advance, there is a slight discount. This is one Christmas party you won't want to miss!

Holiday Lights at Cinderella Castle

Even if you've seen the lights at Cinderella Castle a hundred times, you'll NEVER see them like you will during Christmas at The Magic Kingdom! The Imagineers at Disney take the light spectacular to new levels for the holidays! You'll see thousands of more lights, lots of cool 'wintery' special effects, and even a projection show that decks out the castle to look like a gingerbread castle! You'll also see the spires of Cinderella Castle decked out like candy canes, Christmas presents, and lots more!

Holiday lights at Cinderella Castle

There was also a cool holiday-themed projection show featuring tons of pictures taken throughout the day of families enjoying a magical day at Magic Kingdom!

Cinderella Castle adorned in special Christmas lights!

Events and schedules vary from year to year, but there are always new surprises around every bend and down every path. Surprises and excitement to make your Christmas trip to Magic Kingdom and Walt Disney World a magical adventure!

4) Epcot Christmas

Though far more subtle than the decorations at Magic Kingdom's Main Street, U.S.A., the decorations at Epcot are still beautiful. One of the highlights you'll discover at you approach the International Lagoon is the giant Christmas tree decorated in an international flair (as you would expect).

Epcot's main Christmas tree

You'll also find some pretty cool topiaries, all decked out for the holidays as you explore the paths and walkways of Disney's Epcot. Checkout Goofy and Donald ice skating, and Mickey and Minnie with their Christmas Presents!

This gives just a taste of things to come when you visit the various pavilions of the countries surrounding International Lagoon. You'll also find some nice poinsettia and Christmas topiary displays throughout the park.

Goofy and Donald ice skating at Epcot!

Since Epcot is pretty spread out, be sure you take the time to explore the World Pavilions surrounding the International Lagoon. Otherwise you'll be missing a lot!

Epcot Christmas events

Like Magic Kingdom and the other parks of Walt Disney World, Epcot features special events for the holiday season. However- these events run for a more limited time than those at some of the other parks, so if you're not visiting during these times, you will miss them. Times vary from year to year so check the official Disney site for more info.

Holidays Around The World

If you visit Epcot during the Christmas season, you'll want to be sure to experience "Holidays Around the World" at the international pavilions surrounding the World Showcase Lagoon.

One of Epcot's many Christmas Trees

Each pavilion features Christmas decorations authentic to each country, and each country's version of Santa Claus. From France's Pere Noel (Father Christmas) to Italy's "la Befana" and Norway's Julenissen, each country's pavilion will provide interesting stories and authentic looks at their holiday celebrations.

Epcot's World Pavilions provide a great example of how Christmas is observed in the various countries around the world.

See Santas from around the World

Epcot Candlelight Processional

If you're visiting Disney's Epcot theme park during the Christmas season, be sure to catch Epcot's "Holidays Around The World - Candlelight Processional" held at the American Gardens Theatre in the World Showcase, each day during the holiday season.

Holidays Around the World

The show runs from the day after Thanksgiving until December 30th, and features a variety of guest narrators retelling the story of Christmas each night. This year's narrators include Geena Davis, Neil Patrick Harris, Whoopi Goldberg, and Amy Grant (among others). Check the Disney website to see which of your favorite stars will be the guest narrator during your visit.

There are three shows each night, and each runs about 40 minutes. The shows are included in your park admission price. Much like Epcot's "Fantasmic!" closing show, you'll want to get there early as shows fill up fast and seating is limited.

A visit to the Candlelight Processional is a great way to get in the spirit of the season with your family and friends! In addition to the special guest narrators, the show features a 50-piece orchestra and a mass choir. Chances are that once you've seen the show, you'll want to make it a part of your visit each time you travel to Disney for the holidays.

If you want a guaranteed seat for the show, you can purchase a special Candlelight Dinner Package. The dinner package includes lunch or dinner at a participating Epcot restaurant, seats for the show, and guaranteed fireworks viewing of the IllumiNations: Reflection of Earth closing show.

Guest narrators tell the story of Christmas

Prices vary depending on the restaurant selected. Lunch prices range from about $35-$55 for adults, and dinner prices from $50-$65. If you have one of the deluxe Disney Dining plans, you may be able to use it here, but it will count as two table service meals.

Reservations for the Candlelight Processional dinner packages can be made by calling
(407) WDW-DINE (939-3463).

5) Hollywood Studios Christmas

The giant Hollywood-themed Christmas tree at the entrance to Disney's Hollywood Studios is a sure sign that Christmas is in full swing at Hollywood Studios. The streets are lined with garland and wreaths, the light poles are adorned with stars made of garland and twinkling lights, and there are subtle signs of Christmas everywhere.

Hollywood Studios Christmas tree

Aside from the decorations, things are pretty much the same at Hollywood Studios during Christmas as they are the rest of the year.

Perhaps it's a bit of a disappointment that the park really has only one major event to celebrate the Christmas season, The Osborne Family Spectacle of Dancing Lights, but believe me once you've seen them you'll realize it's a great reason to Visit Hollywood Studios!

Sunset Boulevard decked out for the holidays

The Osborne Family Spectacle of Dancing Lights

Remember back at the beginning of the book where I had a list of reasons why you should and shouldn't visit Disney during the Christmas season? It's really crowded and the weather can be 'iffy'. You may be perfectly warm and comfortable one day, and freeze your butt off the next.

Now, forget all that. There's really only one reason you need to go to Disney World during the holidays. There is one attraction that makes it all worthwhile. One experience above all others that will help your Disney Christmas vacation create memories that last a lifetime. That is the Osborne Family Spectacle of Dancing Lights on the Streets of America at Disney's Hollywood Studios theme park!

Osborne Family Spectacle of Dancing Lights

History of the Osborne Lights

The spectacle that is the Osborne lights began modestly in the mid-1980s as a single family home display in Arkansas. Each year, Jennings Osborne (not Ozzy) and his family would have an annual Christmas display. In just a few years, the display grew and grew until it was too big, and too intrusive to stay in Little Rock. Can you imagine how the neighbors felt having hundreds and hundreds of cars creating gridlock in their neighborhood night after night, year after year? After a court case gained national attention in the mid-90s, Disney offered to move the display to Orlando where it resides today.

The streets are aglow with over 5 million lights!

In the years since it was moved to Disney's Hollywood Studios, the display has continued to grow and has even acquired corporate sponsors like Sylvania to help make it even more spectacular! Each year the display is tweaked, and now contains over 5 million Christmas lights. It was recently upgraded to LED displays to make it even more amazing.

It's snowing at Hollywood Studios!

The Osborne Lights Display

You'll want to head over to The Streets of America section of Hollywood Studios (near the "Lights, Motors, Action!" stunt) show a few minutes before sunset. As dusk arrives the streets come alive with dancing, glistening, wonderful Christmas lights!

Every ½ hour or so, the display transforms from a static display to millions of dancing lights synchronized to Christmas holiday favorites! It's an amazing experience to see the lights synchronized to the music. Up and down the entire street, it's truly a site to behold!

Add in about 30 snow machines 100 or so gallons of liquid snow, and The Osborne Family Spectacle of

Dancing Lights at Disney's Hollywood Studios becomes a Winter Wonderland that you have truly MUST EXPERIENCE!

The lights dance to the music!

6) Animal Kingdom Christmas

Animal Kingdom's main Christmas tree

Although Disney's Animal Kingdom has the fewest signs of Christmas of all the parks at Walt Disney World, it's still a beautiful place to visit during the holiday season. You'll be greeted at the entrance by yet another beautiful Disney Christmas tree. The tree at Animal Kingdom takes on an 'animal' theme. (Of course it does! What else would you expect?)

As you travel throughout the park you'll see Disney's unique approach to Christmas décor throughout. Each shop, trail, and attraction is adorned with beautiful decorations in a classy way without being gaudy or showing any signs of excess. You'll also notice beautiful Christmas displays in many of the shop windows.

Christmas decorations at Animal Kingdom

Animal Kingdom's decorations are unique because they carry a wildlife theme presented throughout the park. This really increases the sense of authenticity you have as you feel you could really be enjoying Christmas in Africa, Asia, or the other lands of Animal Kingdom.

Another great thing about Animal Kingdom is not really unique to the Christmas season, but rather all winter long. With the cooler temperatures, the animals at Kilimanjaro Safaris will be much more active and visible than they are during the summer months. You'll get to see more animals, and they'll likely be closer than they will during the summer months. This will help you get some great wildlife photos on your safari!

You'll get great wildlife photos during the winter months!

Disney Character Greeting Trails

If you explore the various character greeting trails at Camp Minnie-Mickey near the Festival of the Lion King Theater you'll see several unique Disney Christmas trees decorated in a variety of Disney character themes. You'll also notice snow-capped light poles decked out in Christmas garland.

Character-themed Christmas trees at Camp Minnie-Mickey

Be sure to head over to Santa Goofy's Wild Wonderland. Complete with red suit and white beard, Santa Goofy is ready for a unique holiday picture. As you wander the park you'll see many of your favorite Disney characters all decked out in their Christmas attire. You may even spot those crazy chipmunks Chip & Dale! You'll also find strolling musicians around the park throughout the day, entertaining you with holiday favorites.

Meet Goofy, Chip and Dale dressed for the holidays!

Mickey's Jingle Jungle Parade

Mickey's Jingle Jungle Parade is the only special event at Disney's Animal Kingdom theme park during the holiday season. The traditional afternoon jungle parade take on a holiday twist with lively holiday music and your Disney jungle favorites decked out in holiday attire.

Definitely worth checking out if you're in the area around parade time (usually 3:00 p.m.).

Dance to the happy world-beat soundtrack of Mickey's Jingle Jungle Parade as Mickey Mouse and the whole Disney gang join in on a caravan of colors through Disney's Animal Kingdom. Beautiful floats and giant puppets join the Disney pals along the parade route through the park.

7) Disney Gingerbread Houses

A trip to Walt Disney World and the Orlando area during the holiday season would not be complete without checking out some of the gorgeous Gingerbread Houses and other gingerbread displays in and around Disney properties. The houses are a little different each year and are made with hundreds of pounds of real gingerbread and other delectable treats!

Grand Floridian Gingerbread House

The hotels and the WDW Food and Beverage team start baking and assembling the giant houses in early November, and when you see them, you'll see why! These gingerbread creations are not the typical tabletop Gingerbread Houses that you can buy at the local crafts store, these structures can be as high as 15 feet tall-- or more!

Stitch's Boardwalk Bakery – Delicious!

Some of them you can actually walk inside! Here's a look at some of the places to visit to see these incredible, delicious works of art:

- Grand Floridian Hotel – house
- U.S. Pavilion at Epcot – house
- Contemporary - Tree & guard house
- Yacht Club - Train Set
- Beach Club – Carousel
- Boardwalk - Stitch Bakery house

Some of these displays may vary from year to year, so who knows what surprises await you? You can even buy a gingerbread shingle or mini gingerbread house of your very own!

Grand Floridian Gingerbread House

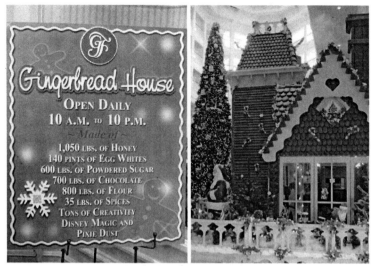

How's that for a recipe??!!

Visit Disney's Grand Floridian hotel during the Christmas season to see one of the MOST AMAZING gingerbread displays you'll EVER see ANYWHERE! Made from over 1,000 lbs. of honey, 600 lbs. of sugar, and 700 lbs. chocolate, this holiday display is sure to stir a craving in any sweet tooth! No tasting allowed!

Disney's Contemporary Resort

Gingerbread tree at Disney's Contemporary Resort

The Contemporary Resort opts for a big Gingerbread Christmas tree rather than the traditional gingerbread house. If a 17 foot tall, 6 foot wide Christmas tree made from 360 eggs, 750 lbs. of flour, and 510 lbs. of honey sounds like a tasty treat, be sure to stop by the Contemporary for a peek at this delectable display!

Other Disney Gingerbread Displays

Visit many of the hotels and you'll find beautiful Christmas displays of gingerbread and lots of other things too. Take a day and explore beyond the parks. You never know what delectable treasures you'll stumble upon!

Gingerbread Carousel at Disney's Beach Club Resort

8) Other Disney Holiday Events

If you're visiting Walt Disney World for the holidays, you may want to check out some of the other holiday events outside the parks. There's always lots to do in the Orlando area, so if you need a break from the hustle and bustle of the theme parks, here are some things you may want to check out...

DisneyQuest New Year's Eve Party

If you're looking for a unique (and FUN!) way to ring in the New Year, check out DisneyQuest's New Year's Eve party! DisneyQuest is an awesome indoor interactive theme park located at Downtown Disney's Westside, right next to Cirque du Soleil.

Check out DisneyQuest's New Year's Eve party

Some people think of DisneyQuest as 'just an arcade', but in reality it is so much more! If you attend the New Year's Eve party at DisneyQuest you'll not only get full access to the traditional arcade games like Pacman, Space Invaders, and Galaga; but you'll also have access to the latest hot games and cool virtual reality experiences like the Virtual Jungle Cruise and Pirates of the Caribbean: Battle for Buccaneer Gold.

There are some other unique activities like CyberSpace Mountain where you can design **and ride** your very own simulated roller coaster and Buzz Lightyear's AstroBlaster where you'll get a chance to drive around your space bumper car and fire your astro-cannon to spin your rivals out of control! Don't forget to visit the Animation Academy where you'll learn to draw your favorite Disney characters during a ½ hour lesson.

Tons of great arcade & virtual reality games!

The DisneyQuest New Year's Eve bash also includes a DJ dance party (party favors included), a New Year's Eve countdown and a confetti drop at midnight. Admission includes a coupon for a free meal at the FoodQuest restaurant on the 5th floor.

Race head-to-head against your friends!

If arcade and virtual reality games are your thing and you're looking for something other than the traditional New Year's Eve party, DisneyQuest may be the place to be!

Festival of the Seasons

Any visit to Walt Disney World is not complete without a trip or two to Downtown Disney. Downtown Disney is a shopping and entertainment complex located just outside the parks. It's divided into three main areas: West Side, Pleasure Island, and Marketplace. The complex includes several Disney-themed gift shops, and several other stores such as a LEGO store and 'Once Upon a Toy'- a really cool toy store containing a variety of classic and contemporary toys.

LEGO store and World of Disney

You'll find lots of restaurants entertainment venues as well. There's a House of Blues, a Planet Hollywood, and Fulton's Crab House among other dining options. You'll also find Cirque du Soleil, DisneyQuest, and an AMC theater complex for your entertainment.

Downtown Disney comes alive for the holidays with its annual 'Festival of the Seasons'. Festival of the Seasons is held annually from mid-November through late-December on the streets of Downtown Disney. Embrace the spirit of the season with the festival's live entertainment including holiday carolers, live Latin, jazz, and pop performances, stilt walkers, and other street performers. There are also lively holiday dance parties with a DJ too.

Inside the World of Disney at Downtown Disney

From the beginning of the festival in mid-November through Christmas Eve, you'll also get a chance to visit with the big man himself when Santa Claus joins the celebration in his Downtown Disney Marketplace chalet! Be sure to bring your Christmas list and smile for your picture with Santa!

From Christmas Day through the end of the festival, you'll get to visit with Santa Goofy instead. (The **real** Santa will be a little busy!)

Meet Santa Claus AND Goofy Claus!

You'll find great places to shop for your unique Disney-themed Christmas gifts too. Be sure to visit Once Upon a Toy, Disney's Days of Christmas, and the World of Disney store to round out your holiday shopping needs.

9) Disney Christmas Magic Awaits

Let the Christmas Memories Begin!

I truly hope you've enjoyed this book and found it to be a useful resource as you plan or consider a holiday vacation to Walt Disney World. I've tried to capture the essence of a Disney Christmas vacation by covering high points while still leaving room for you to discover some of the Disney Christmas magic on your own. Walt Disney World is truly the happiest place on Earth, and whether you've never been to Disney, or if you've been there 20 times, you'll still find lots of new excitement to discover during Christmas at Walt Disney World.

I hope you'll also check out my other Disney books (listed below) which will be excellent resources as you plan your Disney trip for any time of year. If you're just thinking about going and you're wondering what to expect, they'll provide you all the information you need to make the most of your Walt Disney World vacation.

I'd love to hear from you! If you have any questions, concerns, or suggestions, please let me know. You can contact me directly at: Roger@DisneyVacations4Families.com, or you can post a message on my Facebook at: https://www.facebook.com/pages/DisneyVacations4Families/199503310078077?ref=hl. While you're there, please "Like" our page so we can keep you up to date on any changes at the parks, or on any new books or promotions headed your way. Please also check out our website at: www.DisneyVacations4Families.com.

Also by Roger Wilk...

Discover the Magic: Tthe Ultimate Insider's Guide to Walt Disney World

The Ultimate Walt Disney World theme park guide packed with vacation planning and travel tips for Magic Kingdom, Epcot, Hollywood Studios, Animal Kingdom- and even Disney's awesome water parks: Typhoon Lagoon and Blizzard Beach! **Discover the Magic** will guide you every step of the way as you prepare to embark on the trip of a lifetime- an adventure like no other. A magical vacation to Walt Disney World! Discover the Magic today!!!

Disney Tips & Secrets: Unlocking the Magic of a Walt Disney World Vacation

Experience a magical Disney vacation with with over 200 tips and secrets to save time and MONEY while taking the stress out of your Disney vacation. Whether you're going to The Magic Kingdom, Animal Kingdom, Hollywood Studios, or Epcot, we've got you covered! Discover hidden paths and a secret exit from The Magic Kingdom. Beat the crowds as you head for the monorail back to the parking lots or your hotel. Learn the secrets to vacation photos and **so much more!** Get Disney Tips & Secrets today!!!

WAIT- There's one more thing...

If you enjoyed the book, **please** visit Amazon and **post a review**. I'd love to know what you liked about the book and what you didn't like too. Thanks for reading!

###

CPSIA information can be obtained at www.ICGtesting.com
Printed in the USA
BVOW05s1120270414

351747BV00011B/153/P